An Ocean
Called Hope

ALSO BY S.C. FLYNN

The Colour of Extinction
RENARD PRESS, 2024

An Ocean Called Hope

S.C. FLYNN

Downingfield Press | Europe

First published May 2025 by Downingfield Press Europe, an imprint of Downingfield Press Proprietary Limited, Suite 346 / 585 Little Collins Street, Melbourne Victoria 3000, Australia. For a full list of addresses and contact information, visit www.global.downingfield.com

Text copyright © 2025 S.C. Flynn. Typesetting and book design copyright © 2025 Downingfield Press Proprietary Limited. All rights reserved.

Without limiting the rights under copyright reserved above, in accordance with the Copyright Act 1968 (Commonwealth of Australia) no part of this publication may be reproduced, stored in or introduced into a retrieval system, or transmitted, in any form or by any means (electronic, mechanical, xerographic, recording, or otherwise), without the prior written permission of the copyright owner and the publisher of this book, except for brief passages quoted for the purpose of criticism or review.

S.C. Flynn asserts their right to be known as the author of this work.

ISBN 978-1-7635569-5-9 (paperback)

Book and cover design by M. Cheng-Mader.

Downingfield Press undertakes its work on the traditional lands of the Wurundjeri people of the Kulin Nation and pays respect to Elders past, present, and emerging.

DOWNINGFIELD PRESS PROPRIETARY LIMITED
MELBOURNE · LONDON AND MONTRÉAL

 A catalogue record for this work is available from the National Library of Australia

To Claudia

S.C. FLYNN was born of Irish origin in a small Australian town and now lives in Dublin. His poetry has been published in many magazines around the world. His poetry collection *The Colour of Extinction* (Renard Press, October 2024) was *The Observer's* Poetry Book of the Month for October 2024.

Flynn's poetry focuses in part on the natural environment and in part on psychological states, as well as exploring what it means to be returning diaspora Irish. *An Ocean Called Hope* is the fruit of many years of writing and life experience, including living in various countries.

He has been a nature lover since being surrounded by all kinds of creatures in country Australia. S.C. Flynn is also a lifetime jazz musician and singer, having grown up in a musical family. He is married to an Italian and speaks Italian fluently. An obsessive reader, Flynn has always been very happy when surrounded by books.

PART ONE
Memory And Promise   1

PART TWO
Grains   17

PART THREE
Twelve Views Of The Southern Cross   35

PART ONE

MEMORY AND PROMISE

ARRIVALS
Lambay Island, County Dublin

As our boat approached, the shrieking cliffs dissolved
into thousands of fluttering flecks,
each one a bird swirling or huddling,
swooping, bickering or chattering,
living countless rivalries, battles and hopes
on narrow ledges or buffeting winds –
as we have since the sun first hatched, say the gulls –
since before the sky could screech, say the fulmars –
since the sea was a puddle, say the puffins
(though no one trusts their bright-beaked stories).
The slope where we landed was quieter,
with cattle chewing like centuries ago,
but under the gorse lay other Australians
that bounded away and out of sight:
wallabies with tails pumping like crank handles,
descendants of zoo exiles in the eighties
thriving in this new but old home of mine.

RETURN TO ROSCOMMON

So much was lost in the leaving,
in the shuffle of feet to the sea
and the coughs below decks, lost
in the squinting at unimagined sunlight
and the sting of feet on burning sand;
so much I can never regain. Right now
I could be stepping on hungry grass
that cannot harm because unknown to me,
or passing those special places;
wells that could cure the sadness.

NETWORK

The one who arrives is never the same
as the one who left. If this is the end
of a journey I didn't know I was on,
I will never again lose connection.
The fungus underneath my feet stretches
for miles in every direction; neurons
linking tree to tree, forest to forest,
centuries of memories locked in soil,
erupting now and then in domed antennae
to scatter stored-up moments to the wind.

MY CLAN

If I just sit still and listen
to the silence and my heart
I can imagine them all.
Kate stayed on alone for years
gossiping with the shadows
when everyone else had left.
I'm an accidental man, said Thomas
every day of his life as he dug,
an accidental man, that's that.
Deirdre walked around at night
howling at the moon until it howled back;
I can't hear it, but they all could, I'm sure.

MANDATORY POTATO POEM

My grandad dug potatoes for a living
long ago in Australia when he was young,
chiselling them out of the hard-baked soil
then leaving the field each day exhausted
with his back bent as low as the landscape;
resilient and adaptable
like the generations before him,
humble but proud like the potato itself.
A tour guide on the famine ship in Dublin
told us the Irish were known to be tall
because of all the potatoes they ate.
I, six foot three, said: *we are and we do*.

ONE HUNDRED AND SEVENTY YEARS
Carrowbehy Bog, County Roscommon

A lot has happened in five generations,
but nothing can have changed between these hills
that have been holding their breath all that time
and now empty their lungs in this slow, cool breeze
bringing underneath its earthy smell
a fresh hint of the lake that once stood here
and of the glacier that gouged it out
while sliding away in a grinding mime
that left this message: an instant has passed,
no more, and the sun hasn't even blinked.

EIGHTY-FIVE DAYS
Departed 16 January 1849, arrived 11 May 1849

So much she could never remember:
the long, thin evening shadows on the docks of Dublin,
stretched to breaking point towards another world;
the others left behind in ditches,
hands of a hundred wound-down clocks pointing the way,
each frozen forever in its specific moment;
the inland spaces emptied of people
but loaded with future ruins already crumbling;
her birth at the base of a ladder in a hold
dark and pestilent as any afterlife
while the equator slipped under the stern;
the quiet splash – safely out of sight of land, captain –
as her mother's orphaned body met trailing sharks
more honest than those in the workhouse;
the love and sacrifice of nameless women on the lowest bunks
who preserved her; being carried at last
over mudflat shallows to Melbourne,
wiggling her tiny fingers at the dawn.

MULLINGAR WORKHOUSE
Entered 3-4-1846 aged thirteen. Died 4-9-1849.

Any season would do to tell this story.
In summer these structures would gleam defiance,
their dark brown heaviness standing guard
pitiless and immoveable. Even spring
would fail to brighten the picture with its thoughts
 of young life blunted, bent and then ended.
Biting winter makes any scene cruel, but as it happens
I first came here in autumn, so it's easy:
even these buildings look regretful in the rain
and the abandoned graveyard is draped in leaves,
each a memory and promise of rebirth
that the wind will sweep through the rusted gate.

BETWEEN MEATH AND KILDARE

I wander, a solitary forager
like Australia's formidable Bull Ant,
but my mind keeps going back and forth,
asking if life is just a random line
on a map without scale or direction,
as the Royal Canal I'm following
passes from Meath to Kildare and back again.
Maybe these kinds of thoughts were useful once,
when contemplation could find solutions,
but now they are unnecessary tortures
that drive me on with ant-like stings and pincers
through Kildare to Meath and back again.

PASSING MOLERICK BOG

This is a gate to the underworld, they used to say,
and it's easy to think so when the mist floats up at dusk,
a guardian spirit hiding secrets in a cloak,
and the earthy smell grows richer in the dampening air.
Places like this are Ireland's unconscious, storage rooms
lasting millennia, so somewhere down there –
maybe right near the bottom – must be a bit of me
locked in acidic stasis, patiently waiting
while my ancestors left and I at last returned.
I will not go digging, afraid of what I'd find,
as I learnt to think of underworlds as Hell
and I know already how that might feel:
the clawing anguish and need to escape
that leave you gasping for breath, groping for the surface,
desperate to cross back to the other side,
a shattered hermit emerging from seclusion
after battle with the Devil; I hurry on.

SOMEWHERE NEAR MULLINGAR

Somewhere near Mullingar on the third or fourth day,
a thin boy of five or so stood by the road
dropping stones in a famine pot one by one
with a satisfying ping, each metallic plink
raising the level a fraction
like an inverted burial cairn
piled by a dead chieftain's followers.
I was walking to fill in generations,
so I watched while the clangs became clacks
and each falling stone brought a person
gripping the rim with sharp brittle fingers,
lifting themselves out on starvation legs
to join a procession back the way I had come
towards Dublin and wide new continents.
When I looked back, the pot was full and the boy was gone,
so I turned and walked on towards Mullingar.

APRIL 23rd

I must have often walked on death unknowing,
but at Clontarf the mail coat presses my shoulders
as I wade ashore at dawn, spear and shield in hand.
Our fleet's square sails flap behind me in the breeze
while the dragons' eyes seek our enemy
and their little spears that swarm like flies.
By next high tide our leader will be king as promised
or the battle-watchers will have claimed us all;
the water leaves us no retreat, but none is wanted.
Today I weave a strand in history's tapestry.

ON THE FAMINE WAY

My feet started aching just before dark
while evening flattened the shadows into blades
that stabbed the fading day in the back.
By the road lay a tiny pair of shoes;
old, dusty and worn. No one else was there,
so I went on towards the setting sun,
squinting in the glare of discovery,
till something made me turn around and see
a girl of eight or nine, thin and dressed in rags,
step into the shoes. She looked where I was headed –
on to Abbeyshrule, Clondra and Strokestown –
then walked the other way towards Longwood,
Maynooth, Dublin and the ocean called Hope,
leaving no trace, no name, no regrets.

THEIR GIFT OF SILENCE
Rindoon Castle, County Roscommon

This is a special kind of quiet.
The builders always bring their gift of silence,
locking the unwanted language behind stone walls,
from where it shouts for help more and more weakly
until there is no one left to understand it
except those crouching in low turf houses
just out of sight of the stern watchtowers.

No bard ancestor waits for me here;
his voice would mean nothing to me, anyway,
as I brought with me only the builders' words
after three generations far away
that cut me off from the prisoner's roots
so that I do not know exactly what I'm missing,
having only ever heard this silence.

FAMINE VILLAGE

While the rain turns the ground to spotted mud,
I spy a flat stone and jump, balancing,
a sodden flamingo in dark plumage,
teetering in the middle of the mess
when I see a face next to my foot;
not etched or carved, but grown into it:
a man with lines of pain filled with water.

I leap to the next stone and find a girl
of ten or so caught forever mid-scream
and a woman whose thin, compressed agony
sends me rushing faster from stone to stone,
each thrusting its sadness at the sky.

Finally I reach a ruined house and gasp
against the wall as the rain keeps pounding.
At my touch the stones erupt with figures:
the people whose faces I saw below
now writhe and scream as one and then vanish,
leaving me alone, yes really alone
under rain that cleans but doesn't forget.

PART TWO

G R A I N S

REVERSING THE TELESCOPE

Those blissfully cool summer evenings
on our back lawn in small-town Australia,
when the Milky Way was a bright sweep
and individual stars stood out clearly.
Adults, dogs and even kids were quiet;
the crickets were always making their noise
but after a while you didn't notice it,
although you would have if they had stopped.
We looked for constellations and planets
and the first artificial satellites.
Skylab crashed near us not long after this;
we must have seen it up there in its last days.
Dad used to always say after a while:
Wouldn't it be good to have a telescope?
Down there, where the world around me seemed so small,
watching the sky was a sort of dream
of connecting with the world outside.
Now I want to examine the tiniest things,
peering deep inside rather than outwards;
looking back, reversing the telescope.

THE WHEATBIN

When I was five years old or so,
I used to navigate the world
from a large drum that stored wheat
in the backyard of our house,
safe from the roasting sun
under the shadow cast by the fruit trees,
observing the life that swarmed all around,
a whirring universe of sound and colour:
ants and beetles of different kinds,
caterpillars linked together in long chains,
stinging nettles and rye grasses that cut your hands,
clumpy weeds sprouting tall antennae
I used to imagine were military tanks
fighting each other and beaming messages.
Every memory I recover
is another grain added to the bin
that raises me a little higher.

EVENING SONG

Every sunset I watched and listened
to a spectacle that had been going on
long before humans ever reached Australia:
thousands of brightly-coloured parrots
on their way back home after a day foraging,
outlined against the pink and orange sky,
shrieking the language of the continent
and of a primordial era still there.

BRUSH-TAILED LANDLORDS

We shared our house with possums
who lived in the space above the ceiling;
they had been there long before we moved in
and likely regarded us as their tenants.
We kept daylight hours that didn't bother them
and paid the rent by planting fruit trees
that the possums raided every night.
Our orange cats had not signed the lease, though,
and defended their territory,
which led to noisy late-night battles
punctuated by thumps, howls and yowls
that I used to lie awake and listen to;
the two sides were about the same size,
with perfect night vision, claws and fangs.
The descendants of the first landlords
are still there today, fighting to cling on
to a corner of what was once all theirs.

PALEONTOLOGY

A flock of small dinosaurs:
chooks hunting backyard snails,
spearing crunchy shells on sharp beaks
directed by bright orange eyes.
When the heat was too intense
and the whole world sat motionless
waiting for the blissful cool of evening
like the first breath after nearly drowning,
they dug deep holes with scaly feet -
dirt flying up like clouds of flies -
and rested in the cool earth under the surface.
Those that died were buried in the same soil,
bones waiting rediscovery.

CLOUD SPIRITS

The sound of rain on a metal roof,
an orchestra of cloud spirits
drumming just above your head.
The first such night is sleepless,
but then it becomes the most soothing thing
and the rhythm just carries you away.
When that roof was replaced by tiles
that deadened the sound,
Mum kept a large piece of tin
on the ground outside her window
to hear the rain, to dream of the clouds.

SELF-SUFFICIENCY

Dad planted more than twenty fruit trees
to feed his children and to trade:
apples covered with netting,
pears devoured by insects,
oranges the neighbour's chooks roosted in,
lemons with spikes like cats' claws,
peaches raided by possums,
nectarines pecked by birds,
plums made into jam,
apricots in glorious abundance,
mulberries staining everything and everyone.
Mum kept a small garden of cactus
to remind her of the salty, semi-desert region
she grew up in and maybe never really left.

LEGACY

My mother was given some marron –
unfortunately edible crustaceans –
swimming in a plastic bag, claws grasping;
throw them alive in boiling water.
Lacking the neighbours' prey drive,
she led instead a revolt
and set the victims free in a creek.
Mum is no longer here to see them
but the marrons' descendants are still there,
living their lives as she hoped they would.

A VASE FULL OF EYES

Feathers from my grandmother's peacocks
stood on a vase in the sitting room,
watching us with their hundreds of eyes
while they whispered to each other
in silent colourful signs
full of secret meanings and plans.
I was sure that when the door was closed
they flew around like butterflies,
giggling and twittering as they went,
but when I tried to catch them at it
the feathers always dropped in the vase
just in time and stared back mutely at me.

MAGPIE PASS

I still have a scar on my neck
from being attacked by a magpie
while returning from school at nine years old
past a line of trees where they had their nests;
I fled down the road in terror
with the furious bird in pursuit.
Many years later when I went back,
a magpie approached and sung a beautiful song,
a peace offering to make up for Magpie Pass.
I had never blamed them for defending their eggs,
but the song and the peace were lovely.

NUMBAT

Our journey interrupted to watch,
all of us getting out slowly
and staying silent so as not to disturb
a numbat sitting on a log:
the world's cutest anteater,
like a stripy squirrel,
so rare and shy that every sighting is an event.
The forest is still for one long moment
so we can grasp the memory tight
and then the numbat vanishes into the scrub,
leaving us wondering
when the next time would be.

DANCING IN THE DUST

Mr Bedford's shop was a treasure house
of dusty old things on endless shelves.
I used to dream about the gramophone,
imagining people in 1920s clothes
climbing out of the horn to dance the Charleston
by the till to scratchy old records.
Many years later my brother bought the shop
to continue the dancing in the dust.

DESERTED DRIVE-IN

The giant white screen is peeling
and the speaker stands jut out of the concrete
like stunted metal trees gripped by weeds,
their long, thin evening shadows
stretching back towards another time
when people in flares sat in cars
munching crisps and slurping drinks
while movies flashed by and vanished.

COINS

The only collecting I did as a kid
was of coins from all around the world;
I still have them today in an old suitcase.
Anyone who travelled outside Australia
was a target for my pestering
and over time I gathered a metal atlas
that I used to see the world in my mind;
Ireland's harp played a journeying call
and Italian *lire* intrigued me.
None of my coins have any real value,
but that was never the point; they were symbols,
token entrance fees to a festival.

THE COCONUT

There had never been a coconut in our town
until my sister ordered one from the shop.
We waited months for it to arrive
and almost drove Mr Baldini crazy
asking for news of this round messenger
from the outside world we'd never seen.
When the coconut finally arrived,
it was like a taste of the exotic,
a cure for our isolation.
We didn't know what to do with the thing,
so we threw it around for a while
then got a hammer from Dad's toolbox,
sat on the back step and cracked the nut open.
I remember being disappointed,
although I don't know what I expected.
We drank the juice and then each took a spoon,
levered out the flaky white stuff and ate it.
We never talked about the coconut
after we had thrown away the shell;
it had failed to do the impossible.

THE COCOON

I found a cocoon made of twigs
somehow stuck together in a lattice.
I don't know why, but it never opened
and many years later I went away
leaving the cocoon behind on a shelf,
while whatever creature lay inside
never learnt what it truly was.

PART THREE

TWELVE VIEWS OF THE
SOUTHERN CROSS

I. Uluru, central Australia, 1000 BC
You run fast, emu in the sky,
on your long black legs.
In every season
that I've carried my children
behind my husband
you have been above.
And the tree possum
over your head
has watched us
with his hand of shining eyes.
Stay over us, sky emu.
Watch us closely tonight, tree possum.

II. Pythagorean community, southern Italy, 500 BC
The gods have placed the answer in the sky,
low beneath the Centaur's hooves
where the five stars urge a mosaic
of triangles on the eye. He forbade us
to think of those lengths that don't exist
but which I see just above the horizon,
stretching like sacrificial knife blades
from one bright point to another;
others have paid for their seeing with life.
I could strain instead to listen
for the blameless music of the spheres,
but the irrational triangle sides
call me much louder. He told us
that this life is only one of many,
so the price is small as these things go.
I will drink the poison
if you prepare it, but only you.

III. Central India, 1 BC
You must have watched so many battles
dawn, *Trishanku*.
And you know what it means
to want too much;
I'm hanging upside down
between the earth
I took for granted
and the sky I dreamed of reaching.
I've never feared the rolling war dice,
but the wheel of life
is spinning backwards
now, *Trishanku*.

IV. Constantinople, 541 AD
The warm night air is sweet
and sick with sprawling death;
there's no hope above.
Some old pagans placed a cross
below the centaur,
but it must have drifted out of sight
like a gnostic hierarchy.
There's a greater cross on earth by now;
the emperor dragged it from the stars.
But who will stop the plague?

V. Tonga, 800 AD
Take me with you, star duck,
when you fly away down south;
let me fix your broken wing.
I remember watching you
when I was young and dancing
to music so sweet
I couldn't taste the food.
You seemed so close then
but now I wish you were closer;
my grey feathers are ready to fly.

VI. New Zealand, 1200 AD
The heavens need a heavy anchor,
so hold them back, *Te Punga*,
hold back the rushing nights.
Soon the sky boat will carry me off
while I cling to its trailing rope,
but until then, hold it back, *Te Punga*.

VII. Machu Picchu, Peru, 1400 AD
The world of the gods is yours, *Chakana*,
yours and the condor's. Even the mountains
can't lift me out of the puma's paw; up here
where the air is just the sigh of a dream
I'm as far from you as if I crawled in the dust
down in the earthy world of the snake.

VIII. Easter Island, 1500 AD
The five stars tremble through the branches
of the last tree on this island. At dawn,
my loyal axe will cut it down to raise
the final *moai* of my ancestors
and the long gone dead will smile.
But there will be no wood for platforms
to one day lift me huge and rocky
like the eyes that talk to the sky,
my cold stone back to the living sea,
my painted eyes scorching the bare earth.
I tremble, too, but the ancestors call my axe.

IX. Amerigo Vespucci's Ship in the South Atlantic Ocean, 1501 AD
This cross that hangs in godless doubt slid
out of Europe's reach a thousand years ago down
ever deeper into this pagan blackness.
But now it watches as we bring a greater cross
and knows there's nowhere left to hide;
nothing and no one escapes us in the end.

X. Araucania, Chile, 1800 AD
This is no job for the young, *Melipal*;
only old women like me will go on
using one dream to explain another
in this language twisted like dry tree roots.
Your five lights have watched us fight the Incas
and live and trade with the Spanish
and you know I've fought the evil spirits
as well as any *kulku* of the *Mapuche*.
But we both see the invasion coming
and the end of all the old ways;
then not even the dreams will make sense.

XI. Australian Antarctic Territory, last September

While the cross passes over
under bleeding sky signs,
the warming fist of air
presses the ice
till the world's last firstborn
drowns
in the tearful pulse of the juice.

XII. Uluru, central Australia, tomorrow night
The sky kite must be much the same
but looking up has changed;
war in space is the new theology.
Rocket junk floats like so many heresies
and orbiting communication links
have shouted down the angelic orders.
Any old poet who versed to paradise now
would have to dodge the pieces
and when they start shooting
each other's things down with missiles
we'll all end up in inferno.
Every species on earth
is a sacrificial victim
slowly bleeding to death
in the branches of this blurry tree.

www.ingramcontent.com/pod-product-compliance
Lightning Source LLC
Chambersburg PA
CBHW010611100526
44585CB00037B/2508